MESSIAH HIGHLIGHTS
AND OTHER CHRISTMAS MUSIC

MESSIAH
HIGHLIGHTS AND OTHER
CHRISTMAS
MUSIC

A selection of music by HANDEL, BACH, BERLIOZ, BRITTEN, AND OTHERS

Compiled and edited by DAVID WILLCOCKS

THE METROPOLITAN MUSEUM OF ART and
HENRY HOLT AND COMPANY   New York

I am grateful for the valuable assistance of
ALDEN ROCKWELL MURPHY
in the preparation of this volume.

Front jacket: *Virgin and Child with Saint John the Baptist and Angels* (detail)
François Boucher, French, 1703-1770
Oil on canvas, 1765

Gift of Adelaide Milton de Groot, in memory of the de Groot and Hawley families, 1966
66.167

Back jacket: *Virgin and Child in an Apse* (detail)
Workshop of Robert Campin, Flemish, active by 1406, d. 1444
Oil and tempera on canvas, transferred from wood

Rogers Fund, 1905   05.39.2

Published by The Metropolitan Museum of Art, New York, and
Henry Holt and Company, Inc.,
521 Fifth Avenue, New York, New York 10175

Produced by the Department of Special Publications,
The Metropolitan Museum of Art
Designed by Peter Oldenburg
Music engraved by David Budmen, Music Note, Inc., Pitman, New Jersey
Photography by The Metropolitan Museum of Art Photograph Studio
Printed and bound by A. Mondadori, Verona, Italy

LIBRARY OF CONGRESS CATALOGING-IN-PUBLICATION DATA
Messiah highlights and other Christmas music.
    Choruses with acc. originally for orchestra, arr. for piano, and carols
with piano acc.
    Contents: Ev'ry valley shall be exalted; And the glory of the Lord; O
thou that tellest good tidings; [etc.]
    1. Choruses, Sacred, with orchestra – Vocal scores with piano. 2. Orato-
rios – Excerpts – Vocal scores with piano. 3. Carols, English. 4. Christmas
music. I. Willcocks, David, 1919- . II. Handel, George Frideric, 1685-
1759. Messiah. Vocal score. Selections. 1987.
M1999.M53   1987   87-751749
ISBN 0-87099-492-1 (MMA)
ISBN 0-8050-0594-3 (Holt)

10 9 8 7 6 5 4 3 2 1

ISBN 0-8050-0594-3

TABLE OF CONTENTS

INTRODUCTION

THE STORY OF the Infant Jesus, born of a Virgin Mother and worshiped in a lowly stable by Magi led to Bethlehem by a star, has kindled the imagination of poets, musicians, painters, and sculptors for many centuries. Just as some artists have worked on a large scale while others have expressed themselves in miniature, so musicians have responded with works that range from elaborate oratorios to simple carols.

Among the best loved of the large musical works associated with Christmas are George Frideric Handel's *Messiah* (1742), Johann Sebastian Bach's *Christmas Oratorio* (1734), and *L'Enfance du Christ* (1850-1854) by Hector Berlioz. The first part of *Messiah* is devoted to the prophecy of Christ's birth and the fulfillment of that prophecy. Bach's oratorio is a collection of six cantatas to be performed at church services between Christmas and Epiphany. The oratorio by Berlioz describes the flight of the Holy Family into Egypt to escape the wrath of Herod.

Excerpts from these three oratorios are included in this book, as well as a number of carols. Accompanying the music are reproductions of paintings, sculpture, and other works from the collections of The Metropolitan Museum of Art in New York City. Like the music, much of this art celebrates the birth and life of Christ.

It is important to note that a difference exists between the art of the painter and the art of the musician. When a painter has finished his work, his picture will be there for posterity. Although it may require periodic restoration or cleaning, the painting will in essence remain as the artist conceived it. A musical composition, on the other hand, has to be translated into sound before it can be fully appreciated, and the composer remains at the mercy of successive generations of performers who may impose upon the work interpretations that differ widely from each other and from the composer's own conception of his creation.

Handel's *Messiah* is performed today in many different ways, ranging from the singing of favorite airs and choruses by a family gathered round a piano, through "authentic" performances with a small chamber choir and instruments of Handel's period, to the mammoth presentations involving several thousand singers, often supported by a correspondingly large modern orchestra using additional instrumental parts written by Mozart. Whenever, wherever, however *Messiah* is performed, Handel's genius is apparent – the genius recognized by Haydn who said, "He is, indeed, the father of us all"; by Mozart who declared, "Handel understands effect better than any of us'; and by Beethoven who confessed, "I would uncover my head to kneel down on his tomb."

Who can read the phrases "Every valley shall be exalted . . . and the glory of the Lord shall be revealed . . . for unto us a child is born" without thinking of Handel's music to which those words seem indissolubly wed? Composers of lesser stature have been accused of naïveté when they have written descriptive music, but Handel's memorable melodic lines spring naturally from the verbal text:

shall be ex-alt - - - - - - - - ed

the crook-ed__ straight

is ris - en,__ is ris - en__ up - on__thee,__is ris - en

Handel's experience as a composer of opera accounts for his ability to provide dramatic music that matches the mood of the words. Examples abound: the vitality and joy of "For Unto Us a Child Is Born"; the brilliance and splendor of "Glory to God in the Highest," with the distant trumpets proclaiming the arrival of the heavenly host and the strings in their final diminuendo suggesting the return of the angels to heaven; the tranquillity of the pastoral "He Shall Feed His Flock"; and not least, the grandeur of the unison "For the Lord God omnipotent reigneth" amid the exultant cries of "Hallelujah!" It was of the "Hallelujah" chorus that Handel is alleged to have said, when composing it, "I thought I saw all heaven before me, and the great God himself."

If Handel (1685-1759) was the exponent *par excellence* of the dramatic in music, his contemporary, J. S. Bach (1685-1750), epitomized the devotional. A feature of Bach's *Christmas Oratorio,* as of his Passion music and many cantatas, is the inclusion of a number of reflective chorales, the melodies of which would have been familiar to Lutheran congregations. Bach's arrangement of these chorales reveals a vivid imagination, sometimes in the colorful orchestration, but more often in the poignant harmonies. In "Ah! Dearest Jesus, Holy Child," three trumpets seem to hover over the cradle like guardian angels, and in "Break Forth, O Beauteous, Heav'nly Light" there is brilliance in the part-writing and luminosity in the harmonic texture.

Unlike Bach, Hector Berlioz (1803-1869) was

contemptuous of conventional Christianity, but he developed a deep religious instinct, which found expression in his sacred trilogy *L'Enfance du Christ.* "The Shepherds' Farewell," now to be found in the second part of that work, was originally published separately and modestly passed off by the composer as the work of a mythical seventeenth-century musician, Pierre Ducré. Immediately popular, the work has never lost its appeal.

Of the carols included in this book, nearly half are of English origin and described as traditional because neither the authors of the words nor the composers of the melodies can be identified. These traditional carols have been handed down from generation to generation, so it is not surprising that many versions exist of the words and the tunes.

Benjamin Britten (1913-1976), represented in this book by "A New Year Carol," made a valuable contribution to the repertory of twentieth-century Christmas music. In works such as "A Boy Is Born" and "A Ceremony of Carols" the influence of plainsong and medieval polyphony can be detected. Although capable of composing ornate and complex music, Britten responded to the anonymous words of "A New Year Carol" with a setting of exquisite simplicity.

The other carols, drawn from French, German, Dutch, and Basque sources, reflect the range and rich diversity of the music sung at Christmastide. Some, like "Unto Us Is Born a Son" and "Blessed Be That Maid," employ the macaronic form, in which lines of Latin are interspersed with vigorous vernacular phrases; some, such as "The Cherry Tree Carol," are cast in ballad form—that is, they tell a story; while "The Infant King," "A Virgin Most Pure," "King Jesus Hath a Garden," and "The Seven Joys of Mary" have a recurring refrain. Common to all the carols, and to the hymn "As With Gladness," are directness of expression and clarity of structure.

The paintings reproduced in this book range from the rich, majestic pageantry of such fifteenth-century masters as Hans Memling and Giovanni di Paolo to the ebullience of François Boucher in the eighteenth century. A lively millefleurs tapestry decorates "A New Year Carol" and a delicate polychromed wood sculpture accompanies "The Seven Joys of Mary." There are many other reproductions of painting and sculpture, as well as examples of stained glass, manuscript illumination, etching, drawing, and embroidery.

It is my hope that the contents of this book will be as much a joy to the eye as to the ear.

DAVID WILLCOCKS

A NOTE ON THE MUSIC FOR MESSIAH

In the excerpts from *Messiah* selected for this book, type of normal size has been used for all notes written by Handel, and for his indications of tempo, dynamics, and ornamentation. Since he composed at great speed (the first version of *Messiah* was produced in a mere twenty-four days), it is remarkable that he was almost always able to indicate his general intentions. In the cases where, by analogy, additional trills and other notation seem desirable, these have been inserted, but clearly differentiated from Handel's own marks by square brackets [ ] and crossed slurs ⌒ .

The keyboard accompaniment is an almost exact transcription of the original orchestral parts; only rarely has it been necessary to make slight adaptations (generally involving the transposition of one or more notes by an octave) to make the keyboard part easier to play. Handel's accompaniments, particularly of solo airs, sometimes consisted only of a bass line known as the *basso continuo,* it being understood that the keyboard player, often an organist, would provide the necessary additional harmonic support for this line. Continuo players were free to determine the texture and degree of elaboration in their realizations; my own realization, shown by notes in small type in the accompaniment, is but one example.

DW

Highlights from HANDEL'S MESSIAH

EV'RY VALLEY
SHALL BE EXALTED

Isaiah 40:4

G. F. Handel
Tenor solo from *Messiah*

- ed,   shall be ex - alt -   ed,   shall be ex - alt - -

- - - - ed,   and ev' - ry

moun - tain and hill ___ made low: the crook - ed ___ straight,

ev - 'ry val - ley _____ shall _____ be ex - alt - - - - -

[p]

- - ed, and ev - 'ry moun - tain and hill made low:

p

the crook - ed _____ straight, the crook - ed straight, the

crook - ed straight, and the rough pla - ces plain, _____ and the rough pla - ces

AND THE GLORY OF
THE LORD

Isaiah 40:5

G. F. Handel
Chorus from *Messiah*

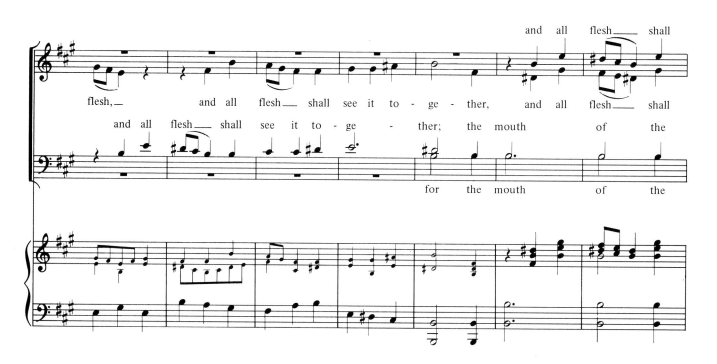

AND THE GLORY OF THE LORD

O THOU THAT TELLEST GOOD TIDINGS

Isaiah 40:9
60:1

G. F. Handel
Alto solo from *Messiah*

ti-dings to Zi - on, get thee up in - to the high moun - tain,

O THOU THAT TELLEST GOOD TIDINGS

O THOU THAT TELLEST GOOD TIDINGS

un- to the ci - ties of Ju - - dah, Be - hold_____ your God!_____ be -

hold your God!_____ be - hold your God!

O thou that tell-est good ti-dings to Zi - on,   a -

rise, shine; for thy light is come,   a - rise,—   a -

rise, ___ a - rise, shine; for thy light is come, and the

[p]

glo - - - - ry of the Lord, the

f

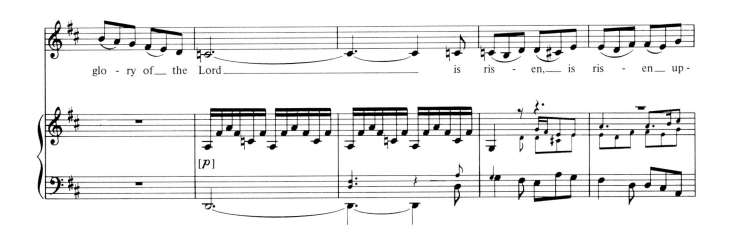

glo - ry of ___ the Lord _____ is ris - en, ___ is ris - en up-

[p]

on ___ thee, ___ is ris ___ - en, is ris ___ - en ___ up - on thee, ___ the ___

glo - ry, the ___ glo - ry, the ___ glo - ry of ___ the Lord ___

D. C. (to page 30)

___ is ris ___ - en ___ up - on thee.

FOR UNTO US
A CHILD IS BORN

Isaiah 9:6

G. F. Handel
Chorus from *Messiah*

FOR UNTO US A CHILD IS BORN

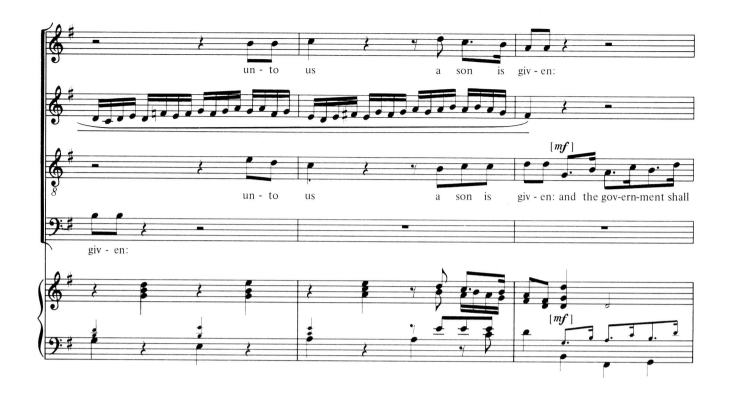

ev - er - last - ing Fa - ther, The Prince of Peace.

ev - er - last - ing Fa - ther, The Prince of Peace.

ev - er - last - ing Fa - ther, The Prince of Peace.

ev - er - last - ing Fa - ther, The Prince of Peace.

GLORY TO GOD
IN THE HIGHEST

Luke 2:14

G. F. Handel
Chorus from *Messiah*

57

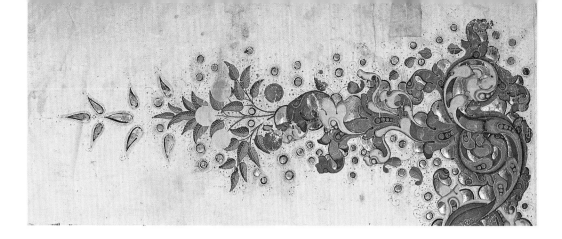

good will,

good will____ to - ward men, to - ward men, good will,

good will____ to - ward men, to-ward men, good will,

good will,

good will, good will, good will____ to - ward men,____

good will, good will, good will to-ward men, good

good will, good will, good will to-ward men,____

good will, good will, good will____ to - ward men,____

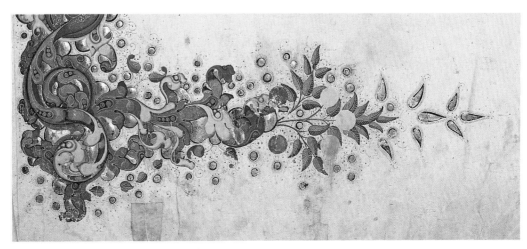

HE SHALL FEED HIS FLOCK

Isaiah 40:11
Matthew 11:28-29

G. F. Handel
Alto and Soprano solos from *Messiah*

Larghetto e piano

He shall feed his flock like a shep - - herd: and he shall ga - ther the lambs with his arm, with his arm.

Deus in ad
iutorium
meum t
intende.

Domine ad adiu
uandum me festina.
Gloria patri et filio
et spiritui sancto.

He shall__ feed his flock like a shep - - herd: and
he__ shall__ ga - ther the lambs__ with__ his arm, with__ his__ arm,
and car - ry____ them____ in his bo - som, and

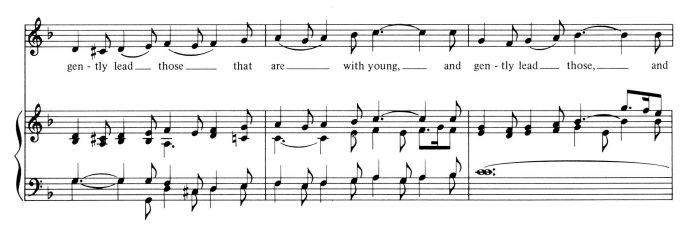

gen - tly lead ____ those ____ that are ____ with young, ____ and gen - tly lead ____ those, ____ and

gen - tly lead ____ those that are ____ with young.

Soprano

Come

un - to___ him,___ all ye that la - bor, come un - to___ him,___ that

are ___ hea - vy la - den,___ and he___ will give___ you rest, come

un - to___ him,___ all ye that la - bor, come un - to___ him, that

are___ hea - vy la - den,___ and he___ will give___ you rest.

Take his yoke up-on you, and learn____ of him; for he____ is____ meek____ and

low - ly of heart: ____ and ye____ shall find rest,____ and ye shall find rest____ un -

to____ your souls, take his yoke up-on you, and

learn____ of him; for he____ is____ meek____ and low - ly of heart:____ and

ye____ shall find rest,____ and ye shall find rest____ un - to____ your souls.

HALLELUJAH

G. F. Handel

Chorus from *Messiah*

Revelation 19:6
11:15
19:16

Selections from CHRISTMAS ORATORIOS AND OTHER HOLIDAY MUSIC

AH! DEAREST JESUS, HOLY CHILD

J. S. Bach
from the *Christmas Oratorio*

Translated by
the Reverend John Troutbeck

Ah! dear - est Je - sus,— ho - ly child,

BREAK FORTH, O BEAUTEOUS, HEAV'NLY LIGHT

Translated by
the Reverend John Troutbeck

J. S. Bach
from the *Christmas Oratorio*

Break forth, O beauteous, heav'nly light, And usher in the morning;
Ye shep-herds, shrink not with af-fright, But hear the an-gel's warn - ing.

This child, now weak in in-fan - cy, Our con-fi-dence and joy shall be,

The pow'r of Sa - tan break - ing, Our peace e - ter-nal mak - ing.

A NEW YEAR CAROL

Words anonymous

Benjamin Britten

Quietly

pp

p

1. Here we bring new wa - ter from the
2. Sing __ reign of Fair __ Maid, with
3. Sing __ reign of Fair __ Maid, with

3rd verse to ⊕
(v. 3 ═══ *)*

well __ so clear,   For to wor-ship God with, this   hap-py New   Year.
gold up-on her toe,   O-pen you the West Door, and   turn the Old Year   go. } *Sing*
gold up-on her chin,   O-pen you the East Door, and   let the New Year   in.

(v. 3 ═══ *)*

THE SHEPHERDS' FAREWELL

Translated by Paul England

Hector Berlioz
from *L'Enfance du Christ*
(slightly adapted)

Allegretto

p 1. Thou must leave thy low - ly
p 2. Bless - ed Je - sus, we im -
pppp 3. Blest are ye be - yond all

dwell - ing, The hum - ble crib, the sta - ble bare, Babe, all mor - tal
plore thee, With hum - ble love and ho - ly fear, In the land that
mea - sure, Thou hap - py fa - ther, mo - ther mild! Guard ye well your

poco f

babes ex - cell - ing, Con - tent our earth - ly lot to share.
lies be - fore thee, For - get not us who lin - ger here!
heav'n - ly trea - sure, The Prince of Peace, the Ho - ly Child!

* Small notes are alternatives for 1st and 2nd basses.

94

96   THE SHEPHERDS' FAREWELL

BLESSED BE THAT MAID

Words by George R. Woodward

English traditional

1. Bless-ed be_ that maid Ma-rie; Born_ he was_ of_
2. In_ a man-ger of an ass_ Je-su lay_ and_

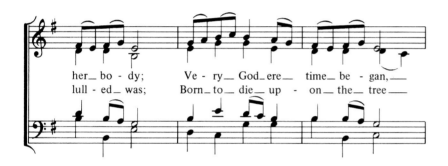

her_ bo-dy; Ve-ry_ God_ ere_ time_ be-gan,_
lull-ed_ was; Born_ to die_ up-on_ the_ tree_

REFRAIN

Born_ in_ time the_ Son_ of Man._ E - ya!_ Je-sus
Pro-pec-can-te_ ho-mi-ne._

ho-di-e_____ Na-tus_ est_ de_ vir-gi-ne.

3. Sweet and blissful was the song
   Chanted of the angel throng,
   "Peace on earth," Alleluya.
   In excelsis gloria.
     Eya!, etc.

4. Fare three kings from far-off land,
   Incense, gold, and myrrh in hand;
   In Bethlem the babe they see,
   Stellae ducti lumine.
     Eya!, etc.

5. Make we merry on this fest,
   In quo Christus natus est;
   On this child I pray you call
   To assoil and save us all.
     Eya!, etc.

KING JESUS HATH A GARDEN

Translated by George R. Woodward

Dutch traditional

1. King Je-sus hath_ a gar-den full of di-vers_ flow'rs, Where I go cull-ing
2. The li-ly, white_ in blos-som there, is cha-sti-ty: The vi-o-let,_ with

po-sies gay, all times_ and_ hours.
sweet_ per-fume, hu-mi-li-ty.

REFRAIN

There_ naught is heard but pa-ra-dise bird, Harp,

3. The bonny damask-rose is known as patïence:
   The blithe and thrifty marygold, obedïence.

   There naught is heard, etc.

4. The crown imperial bloometh too in yonder place,
   'Tis charity, of stock divine, the flower of grace.

   There naught is heard, etc.

5. Yet, 'mid the brave, the bravest prize of all may claim
   The star of Bethlem—Jesus—blessèd be his name!

   There naught is heard, etc.

6. Ah! Jesu Lord, my heal and weal, my bliss complete,
   Make thou my heart thy garden plot—fair, trim, and neat.

   That I may hear this musick clear:
   Harp, dulcimer, lute,
   With cymbal, trump, and tymbal,
   And the tender, soothing flute.

A VIRGIN MOST PURE

English traditional

1. A Virgin most pure as the prophets do tell, Hath brought forth a baby, as it hath befell; To be our Redeemer from death, hell, and sin, Which Adam's transgression had wrapped us in.

2. In Bethlehem Jewry a city there was, Where Joseph and Mary together did pass, And there to be taxed with many one mo, For Caesar commanded the same should be so.

3. Then they were constrain'd in a stable to lie, Where horses and asses they used for to tie; Their lodging so simple they took it no scorn, But against the next morning our Savior was born.

4. Then presently after the shepherds did spy A number of angels that stood in the sky; They joyfully talked and sweetly did sing, "To God be all glory our heavenly King."

For refrain, please turn the next page.

Aye, and there - fore_ be_ mer - ry; Re -

joice,_ and be_ you mer - ry; Set_

sor - row_ a - side; Christ_ Je - sus_ our_

Sa - vior was born at_ this tide.

UNTO US IS BORN A SON

Translated by George R. Woodward

Tune from *Piae Cantiones*, 1582

1. Un-to us is born a son, King of quires su - per - nal: See on earth his
2. Christ, from heav'n de - scend-ing low, Comes on earth a stran - ger; Ox and ass their

life be - gun, Of lords the Lord e - ter - nal, Of lords the Lord e - ter - nal.
own - er know, Be - cra - dled in the man - ger, Be - cra - dled in the man - ger.

3. This did Herod sore affray,
   And grievously bewilder,
   So he gave the word to slay,
   And slew the little childer,
   And slew the little childer.

4. Of his love and mercy mild
   This the Christmas story;
   And O that Mary's gentle child
   Might lead us up to glory,
   Might lead us up to glory.

5. O and A, and A and O,
   Cum cantibus in choro,
   Let our merry organ go,
   Benedicamus Domino,
   Benedicamus Domino.

THE INFANT KING

1. Lul - la - by ba - by, now__ re - clin - ing,
2. Lul - la - by ba - by, now__ a - sleep - ing,
3. Lul - la - by ba - by, now__ a - doz - ing,
4. Lul - la - by! is__ the babe a - wak - ing?

Sing lul - la - by! ... *Sing lul - la - by!*

Hush, do not wake the In - fant King. An - gels are watch - ing, stars are
Hush, do not wake the In - fant King. Soon will come sor - row with the
Hush, do not wake the In - fant King. Soon comes the cross,__ the nails, the
Hush, do not stir the In - fant King, Dream - ing of Eas - ter, glad - some

shin - ing, O - ver the place__ where he__ is ly - ing:
morn - ing, Soon will come bit - ter grief__ and weep - ing:
pierc - ing, Then in the grave__ at last__ re - pos - ing:
morn - ing, Con - quer - ing death,__ its bond - age break - ing:

Sing__ lul - la - by!

Sing lul - la - by!

THE INFANT KING   105

IN DULCI JUBILO

Translated by Robert Lucas Pearsall

German traditional

1. *In dul - ci ju - bi - lo* ___ Let__ us our hom - age shew; ___
2. *O Je - su par - vu - le,* ___ I yearn for thee__ al - way, ___

Our heart's joy ___ re - clin ___ eth *In___ prae - se - pi - o,* ___ And
Hear me, I ___ be - seech ___ thee, *O Puer op - ti - me,* ___ My

like ___ a bright ___ star shin - eth, *Ma - tris ___ in gre - mi - o.* ___
pray - er let ___ it reach thee, *O Prin - ceps glo - ri - ae.* ___

Al - pha es ___ et O! ___ *Al - pha es ___ et O!* ___
Tra - he me ___ post te! ___ *Tra - he me ___ post te!* ___

3. O | Patris cari | tas!
   O | Nati leni | tas!
   | Deeply were we | stainèd
   Per | nostra crimi | na;

But | thou hast for us | gainèd
Coe | lorum gaudi | a.
| O that we were | there,
| O that we were | there!

4. U | bi sunt gaudi | a,
   If | that they be not | there?
   | There are angels | singing
   | Nova canti | ca,

| There the bells are | ringing
In | regis curi | a.
| O that we were | there,
| O that we were | there!

* Vertical lines indicate bar lines; strong beat follows bar line.

HE IS BORN THE DIVINE CHRIST CHILD
IL EST NE LE DIVIN ENFANT

Translated by David Willcocks

French traditional

1. More than four thou-sand years on earth, Man a-wait-ed this joy-ous birth.
3. In a man-ger thou deignst to be, For a God, what hu-mi-li-ty!

D.S.

1. De - puis plus de qua - tre mille ans Nous at - ten - dions cet heur - eux temps.
3. Une é - ta - ble est son lo - ge - ment, Pour un Dieu quel a - bais - se - ment!

Sop.

2. O what beau - ty and charm are thine, Heav'n-ly grace to our hearts sup-ply-ing;
4. Je - su, King, whom we bow be - fore, Yet an in - fant, all power de - ny-ing;

Alto

2. Ah! qu'il est beau, qu'il ___ est char - mant, Ah! que ses grâ - ces ___ sont par - fai - tes;
4. O Jé - sus, roi ___ tout puis - sant, Si pe-tit en - fant ___ que vous ê - tes;

2. O what beau - ty and charm are thine, O what sweet - ness thou Child di - vine!
4. Je - su, King, whom we bow be - fore, Rule our hearts now and ev - er - more.

D.S.

2. Ah! qu'il est beau, qu'il ___ est char - mant, Qu'il est doux ce di - vin en - fant!
4. O Jé - sus, roi ___ tout puis - sant, Rég - nez sur nous en - tiè - re - ment.

THE SEVEN JOYS OF MARY

English traditional

Sopranos

1. The first good joy that Ma - ry had, It was the joy of one;

All

To see the bless - ed Je - sus Christ, When he was first her son:

When he was first her son, good Lord; And bless - ed may he be:

REFRAIN

Praise Fa - ther, Son, and Ho - ly Ghost To all e - ter - ni - ty.

2. The next good joy that Mary had,
It was the joy of two;
To see her own son Jesus Christ
Making the lame to go:
Making the lame to go, good Lord,
And happy may we be:
Praise Father, etc.

3. The next good joy that Mary had,
It was the joy of three;
To see her own son Jesus Christ
Making the blind to see:
Making the blind to see, good Lord,
And happy may we be:
Praise Father, etc.

4. The next good joy that Mary had,
It was the joy of four;
To see her own son Jesus Christ
Reading the bible o'er:
Reading the bible o'er, good Lord,
And happy may we be:
Praise Father, etc.

5. The next good joy that Mary had,
It was the joy of five;
To see her own son Jesus Christ
Bringing the dead alive:
Bringing the dead alive, good Lord,
And happy may we be:
Praise Father, etc.

6. The next good joy that Mary had,
It was the joy of six;
To see her own son Jesus Christ
Upon the crucifix:
Upon the crucifix, good Lord,
And happy may we be:
Praise Father, etc.

7. The next good joy that Mary had,
It was the joy of seven;
To see her own son Jesus Christ
Ascending into heaven:
Ascending into heaven, good Lord,
And happy may we be:
Praise Father, etc.

AS WITH GLADNESS

Words by William Chatterton Dix

Abridged from a chorale by
Conrad Kocher

OPTIONAL DESCANT

1. As with gladness men of old Did the guiding star behold,
2. As with joyful steps they sped To that lowly manger-bed,

As with joy they hailed its light, Leading onward, beaming bright,
There to bend the knee before Him whom heav'n and earth adore,

So, most gracious God, may we Evermore be led to thee.
So may we with willing feet Ever seek thy mercy-seat.

3. As they offered gifts most rare
   At that manger rude and bare,
   So may we with holy joy,
   Pure, and free from sin's alloy,
   All our costliest treasures bring,
   Christ, to thee our heav'nly King.

4. Holy Jesu, every day
   Keep us in the narrow way;
   And, when earthly things are past,
   Bring our ransomed souls at last
   Where they need no star to guide,
   Where no clouds thy glory hide.

5. In the heav'nly country bright
   Need they no created light;
   Thou its light, its joy, its crown,
   Thou its sun which goes not down:
   There forever may we sing
   Alleluyas to our King.

112

TOMORROW
SHALL BE MY DANCING DAY

English traditional

1. To-mor-row shall be___ my danc-ing day; I would___ my true___ love did___ so chance To___
2. Then was___ I born of a Vir-gin pure, Of her___ I took___ flesh-ly___ sub-stance, Thus___
3. In a man-ger laid___ and wrapp'd___ I was, So ve-ry poor,___ this was___ my chance, Be -

see the le-gend of___ my play, To call___ my true___ love to___ my dance.
was I knit___ to man's___ na-ture, To call___ my true___ love to___ my dance. *Sing oh! my___*
twixt an ox and a sil-ly poor ass, To call___ my true___ love to___ my dance.

To___ see the
Thus___ was I
Be - twixt an

love, oh!___ my love, my love, my

love; This___ have I done___ for my___ true love.

THE CHERRY TREE CAROL

English traditional

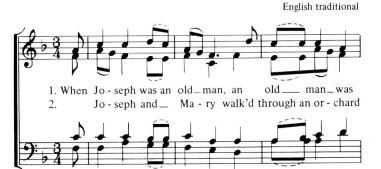

1. When Jo-seph was an old—man, an old—man—was
2. Jo-seph and—Ma-ry walk'd through an or-chard

he, He—mar-ried Vir-gin Ma-ry, the—
green, There were ber-ries and—cher-ries as—

Queen—of Ga-li-lee, He—mar-ried Vir-gin
thick—as may be seen, There were ber-ries and—

Ma-ry,—the Queen—of Ga-li-lee.
cher-ries—as thick—as may be seen.

3. And | Mary spoke to | Joseph,
   So | meek and so | mild,
   "Joseph, | gather me some | cherries,
   For | I am with | child,
   Joseph, | gather me some | cherries,
   For | I am with | child."

4. And | Joseph flew in | anger,
   In | anger flew | he,
   "Let the | father of the | baby
   Gather | cherries for | thee,
   Let the | father of the | baby
   Gather | cherries for | thee."

5. Then | up spoke baby | Jesus
   From | in Mary's | womb,
   "Bend | down the tallest | tree
   That my | mother might have | some,
   Bend | down the tallest | tree
   That my | mother might have | some."

6. And | bent down the tallest | branch
   Till it | touched Mary's | hand,
   Cried | she, "Oh, look thou | Joseph,
   I have | cherries by com|mand,"
   Cried | she, "Oh, look thou | Joseph,
   I have | cherries by com|mand."

* Vertical lines indicate bar lines; strong beat follows bar line.

115

LIST OF ILLUSTRATIONS

Page 38: *The Annunciation* (detail)
Albrecht Dürer, German, 1471-1528
Woodcut, 1511

Rogers Fund, 1918   18.65.16

Page 39: *Virgin and Child*
Initial "S" from a manuscript illumination
Probably a follower of Stefano da Zevio,
Italian (Veronese)
Ink, tempera, and gold leaf on vellum,
ca. 1425

Rogers Fund, 1912   12.56.2

Page 40: Decorative border
Detail (top border) of an illuminated
manuscript page depicting *The
Annunciation,* from the *Belles Heures* of
Jean, Duc de Berry, folio 30
Pol, Jean, and Herman de Limbourg, French
(Parisian)
Tempera and gold leaf on vellum, ca. 1406-09

The Cloisters Collection, 1954   54.1.1

Pages 42, 43: Decorative borders
Detail from a page of the *Horae in Laudem
Beatissimae Virginis Mariae, ad usum
Romanum*
Paris: Simon Colines, 1543

Harris Brisbane Dick Fund, 1924   24.49.10

Page 45: *The Adoration of the Magi*
Quentin Massys, Flemish, 1465/66-1530
Tempera and oil on wood, 1526

John Stewart Kennedy Fund, 1911   11.143

Pages 46, 47: Decorative borders
Detail (side border) of an illuminated
manuscript page depicting *The Flight into
Egypt,* from the *Belles Heures* of Jean,
Duc de Berry, folio 63
Pol, Jean, and Herman de Limbourg, French
(Parisian)
Tempera and gold leaf on vellum, ca. 1406-09

The Cloisters Collection, 1954   54.1.1

Page 49: *Two Winged Putti*
François Boucher, French, 1703-1770
Black chalk and gray wash, heightened with
white, on beige paper

Gift of Charles K. Lock, 1960   60.175.1

Page 52: *Angel, The Annunciation,* and *The
Nativity*
Detail of a reliquary shrine of the Virgin and
Child, believed made for Queen Elizabeth
of Hungary
French (possibly Parisian), ca. 1340
Silver gilt and translucent enamel

The Cloisters Collection, 1962   62.96

Page 55: *Madonna and Child with Angels*
Pietro di Domenico da Montepulciano,
Italian (School of the Marches), active first
quarter 15th century
Tempera on wood, gold ground

Rogers Fund, 1907   07.201

Page 56: *Madonna and Child Enthroned, with
Saints*
Raphael, Italian (Umbrian), 1483-1520
Tempera, oil, and gold on wood

Gift of J. Pierpont Morgan, 1916   16.30a,b

Page 57: God the Father
Detail from *The Annunciation*
Martin Schongauer, German, 1450(?)-1491
Engraving, ca. 1484

Harris Brisbane Dick Fund, 1932   32.64.1

Page 58: Palmette and rosette border
Pot-metal glass
French (possibly Abbey of St.-Rémy at
Reims), ca. 1200

The Cloisters Collection, 1978   1978.408.2

Page 59: Hand of God with two censing
angels
Plaque from a châsse
North Spanish, late 11th century
Champlevé enamel on copper gilt

Gift of J. Pierpont Morgan, 1917   17.190.687

Pages 60, 61: Decorative borders
Detail (bottom border) of an illuminated page
from a choir book
Italian (probably Florentine), mid-15th
century
Tempera and gold leaf on parchment

Gift of Louis L. Lorillard, 1896   96.32.16

Page 62: *Heavenly Host*
Detail of an illuminated manuscript page
from the *Belles Heures* of Jean, Duc de Berry,
folio 218
Pol, Jean, and Herman de Limbourg, French
(Parisian)
Ink, tempera, and gold leaf on vellum,
ca. 1406-09

The Cloisters Collection, 1954   54.1.1

Page 63: *Infant Joy* (detail)
Page from *Songs of Innocence and Experience,*
1794 (1825 printing)
William Blake, British, 1757-1827
Relief etching, hand-painted with watercolor
and gold

Rogers Fund, 1917   17.10.25

Page 64: *The Adoration of the Magi*
Illuminated manuscript page from the *Belles
Heures* of Jean, Duc de Berry, folio 54v
Pol, Jean, and Herman de Limbourg, French
(Parisian)
Ink, tempera, and gold leaf on vellum,
ca. 1406-09

The Cloisters Collection, 1954   54.1.1

Page 65: Decorative border
Detail from a page of the *Horae in Laudem
Beatissimae Virginis Mariae, ad usum
Romanum*
Paris: Simon Colines, 1543

Harris Brisbane Dick Fund, 1924   24.49.10

Page 66: *Angel with a Banderole*
Camillo Procaccini, Italian, ca. 1555-1629
Red chalk and red wash, heightened with
white, on beige paper

Harry G. Sperling Fund, 1976   1976.186

Page 67: *God the Father and Angels Adoring the
Christ Child*
Giovanni Benedetto Castiglione, Italian,
1609-1670
Etching
Purchase, Joseph Pulitzer Bequest, 1917   17.50.17(48)

Page 68: *Virgin and Child with the Cat; and
Joseph at the Window*
Rembrandt, Dutch, 1606-1669
Etching, 1654

Purchase, Gift of Henry Walters, by exchange, 1923
23.51.5

Page 69: Decorative border
Detail (side border) of an illuminated
manuscript page depicting the *Heavenly
Host,* from the *Belles Heures* of Jean,
Duc de Berry, folio 218
Pol, Jean, and Herman de Limbourg, French
(Parisian)
Tempera and gold leaf on vellum, ca. 1406-09

The Cloisters Collection, 1954   54.1.1

Page 70: *Virgin and Child*
Attributed to Claux de Werve, French
(Burgundian)
From the Convent of the Poor Clares, Poligny
Polychromed and gilded limestone,
ca. 1415-17

Rogers Fund, 1933   33.23

Page 71: *The Annunciation to the Shepherds*
Detail of an illuminated manuscript page
from *The Apocalypse*, folio 1v
Tempera, gold, and silver on vellum
Norman (Coutances), first quarter 14th
century

The Cloisters Collection, 1968   68.174

Page 72: Musical putti
Detail from *Rest on the Flight into Egypt*
Lucas Cranach the Elder, German, 1472-1553
Woodcut

Gift of Felix M. Warburg and his family, 1941   41.1.159

Page 73: *The Nativity*
Detail of a crèche
Italian (Neapolitan), 18th century
Figures of polychromed terra-cotta and wood,
with silk robes and silver gilt

Gift of Loretta Hines Howard, 1964   64.164.1-167

Pages 74, 75: Decorative borders
Details (top and bottom borders) of an
illuminated page from a choir book
German (probably Mainz), second quarter
15th century
Tempera and ink on parchment

Gift of Alice M. Dike, in memory of her father,
Henry A. Dike, 1928   28.225.3

Page 76: Flying putti
Detail from *Rest on the Flight into Egypt*
Lucas Cranach the Elder, German, 1472-1553
Woodcut

Gift of Felix M. Warburg and his family, 1941   41.1.159

Page 77: *The Holy Family with Saints Francis,
Anne, and the Infant Saint John the Baptist*
Workshop of Peter Paul Rubens, Flemish,
1577-1640
Oil on canvas

Gift of James Henry Smith, 1902   02.24

Pages 78, 79: Decorative borders
Detail from a page of the *Horae in Laudem
Beatissimae Virginis Mariae, ad usum
Romanum*
Paris: Simon Colines, 1543

Harris Brisbane Dick Fund, 1924   24.49.10

Pages 80, 81: Decorative borders
Detail (bottom border) of an illuminated
manuscript page depicting *The Nativity*,
from the *Belles Heures* of Jean, Duc de Berry,
folio 48v
Pol, Jean, and Herman de Limbourg, French
(Parisian)
Tempera and gold leaf on vellum, ca. 1406-09

The Cloisters Collection, 1954   54.1.1

Page 82: *Adoration of the Magi*
Detail of a portable altar depicting scenes
from the life of Christ
Rhenish (Cologne), ca. 1150-60
Champlevé enamel on copper gilt

Gift of J. Pierpont Morgan, 1917   17.190.410-413

Page 83: *The Adoration of the Magi*
Giovanni di Paolo, Italian (Sienese), active by
1420, d. 1482
Tempera and gold on wood

The Jack and Belle Linsky Collection, 1982   1982.60.4

Pages 84, 85: Dress border (detail)
Undyed linen embroidered in silk
Greek Isles (Crete), 18th century

Bequest of Richard Berry Seager, 1925   26.34.4

Page 86: Decorative border
Detail from a page of the *Horae in Laudem
Beatissimae Virginis Mariae, ad usum
Romanum*
Paris: Simon Colines, 1543

Harris Brisbane Dick Fund, 1924   24.49.10

Page 87: *Nativity with the Annunciation to the
Shepherds*
Follower of Jan Joest of Calcar, Flemish,
active ca. 1515
Oil on wood

The Jack and Belle Linsky Collection, 1982   1982.60.22

Page 88: *Virgin and Child*
Dieric Bouts, Flemish, active by 1457,
d. 1475
Tempera and oil on wood

Bequest of Theodore M. Davis, 1915, Theodore M. Davis
Collection   30.95.280

Page 91: *Virgin and Child with Saint John the
Baptist and Angels* (detail)
François Boucher, French, 1703-1770
Oil on canvas, 1765

Gift of Adelaide Milton de Groot, in memory of the
de Groot and Hawley families, 1966   66.167

Page 92: *A Hawking Party* (detail)
Wool tapestry
South Netherlandish, early 16th century

Gift of George Blumenthal, 1941   41.100.195

Page 94: Two musicians
Detail of a page from a psalter and prayer book
made for Bonne of Luxembourg, Duchess
of Normandy
Atelier of Jean le Noir, French (Parisian)
Tempera, grisaille, and gilt on vellum,
ca. 1345

The Cloisters Collection, 1969   69.86

Page 95: *The Adoration of the Shepherds*
Central panel of a triptych
Gerard David, Flemish, active by 1484,
d. 1523
Tempera and oil on wood

Bequest of Michael Friedsam, 1931, The Friedsam
Collection   32.100.40a

Page 97: *Virgin and Child*
Style of Jan van Eyck, Flemish, third quarter
15th century
Tempera and oil on wood

Gift of Henry G. Marquand, 1889, Marquand
Collection   89.15.24

Page 98: Angel and cupid
Detail from *Musical Garden Party*
English, third quarter 17th century
Colored silk on canvas

Gift of Irwin Untermyer, 1964   64.101.1314

Page 99: *Music-Making Angels*
Albrecht Dürer, German, 1471-1528
Pen and brown ink

Gift of Mrs. William H. Osborn, 1961   61.257

Page 101: *The Virgin of the Nativity*
Filippino Lippi, Italian (Florentine), probably
b. 1457, d. 1504
Fragment of a painting in tempera and gold
on wood

Gift of Donald S. Klopfer, 1982   1982.73

Page 102: *Virgin and Child in an Apse* (detail)
Workshop of Robert Campin, Flemish, active
by 1406, d. 1444
Oil and tempera on canvas, transferred from
wood

Rogers Fund, 1905   05.39.2

Page 103: *Virgin and Child*
Hans Memling, Flemish, active ca. 1465,
d. 1494
Tempera and oil on wood

Bequest of Michael Friedsam, 1931, The Friedsam
Collection   32.100.59

Page 104: *The Nativity*
Lorenzo Monaco, Italian (Florentine),
    b. ca. 1370, d. 1425
Tempera on wood, gold ground

Robert Lehman Collection, 1975   1975.1.66

Page 105: Decorative borders
Details from a page of the *Horae in Laudem
    Beatissimae Virginis Mariae, ad usum
    Romanum*
Paris: Simon Colines, 1543

Harris Brisbane Dick Fund, 1924   24.49.10

Page 107: *Madonna and Child in a Niche*
Luca della Robbia, Italian (Florentine),
    1399/1400-1482
Enameled terra-cotta

Bequest of Susan Dwight Bliss, 1966   67.55.98

Page 109: *The Nativity*
Workshop of Fra Angelico, Italian
    (Florentine)
Tempera and gold on wood, ca. second quarter
    15th century

Gift of May Dougherty King, 1983   1983.490

Page 110: Decorative border
Detail (bottom border) of an illuminated page
    from a choir book
Attributed to Francesco d'Antonio del Cherico
    and associates, Italian (Florentine)
Tempera and gold leaf on parchment, third
    quarter 15th century

Gift of Louis L. Lorillard, 1896   96.32.8

Page 111: *Virgin and Child*
German (Rhenish or Bohemian), first quarter
    15th century
Polychromed and gilded wood

Anonymous Loan

Page 113: *The Nativity and
    the Annunciation to the Magi*
Detail from the central panel of *The Nativity*
    altarpiece
Workshop of Rogier van der Weyden,
    Flemish, b. 1399/1400, d. 1464
Tempera and oil on wood

The Cloisters Collection, 1949   49.109

Page 114: *Virgin and Child*
German, 15th century
Hand-colored woodcut

Gift of Felix M. Warburg and his family, 1941   41.1.40

Page 115: *Holy Family*
South German (School of Ulm), ca. 1500
From the church at Gutenzell, Oberamt
    Biberach, Württemberg
Polychromed and gilded wood

Gift of Alastair B. Martin, 1948   48.154.1

Page 120: *Angel with Trumpets*
Luca Cambiaso, Italian (Genoese), 1527-1585
Pen and bistre

Robert Lehman Collection, 1975   1975.1.283

Endleaves: *Dante and Beatrice with the Blessed
    Souls*
Woodcut from *Comedia dell'Inferno, del
    Purgatorio, & del Paradiso*
Canto 27 of *Paradiso,* by Dante Alighieri
Venice: Published by Giovambattista Marchiò
    Sessa et Fratelli, 1578

Gift of Francis Leonard Cater, 1958   58.584

Cover stamping: Trumpeter
Ornamental design from *Daniel's Copy-Book*
London: 1664

Harris Brisbane Dick Fund, 1942   42.69.2

INDEX OF FIRST LINES